Empowering Persons With Disabilities 2.0

A guide for service delivery to hearing impaired and limited English proficiency (LEP) clients

Richard Dicks, Jr.

Empowering Persons With Disabilities 2.0
is © 2021 Richard Dicks, Jr.

Manufactured in the United States of America

ISBN: 978-1-886591-28-8

Published for Mr. Dicks by
BLUE CREEK PRESS
Heron, Montana 59844
books@bluecreekpress.com
Editing, proofing and design
provided by Blue Creek Press

Table of Contents

Carefully watch your thoughts, for they become your words. Manage and watch your words, for they will become your actions. Consider and judge your actions, for they become your habits. Acknowledge and watch your habits, for they shall become your values. Understand and embrace your values, for they become your destiny.

Mahatma Ghandi

Introduction

This guide offers a slightly different service model from my first guide, and includes sensory disabilities such as Blind/Low Vision and Deaf and Hard-of-Hearing. The methods of administration in my previous guide establish a blueprint of how to provide accurate, timely and effective communication for persons with disabilities.

In this guide, *Empowering Persons with Disabilities 2.0: A Guide for Deaf and Hard-of-Hearing and LEP Service Delivery Models,* I will discuss the legal aspects distinguishing laws governing Language Access for federally conducted and federally assisted programs under Title VI of the Civil Rights Act of 1964 from the Americans with Disabilities Act (ADA) of 1990 and Amendments of 2008 and the Rehabilitation Act of 1973, which affords protection to the Deaf and Hard-of-Hearing to prevent discrimination.

Since our laws are ever-changing, it is critical to distinguish the ADA/504 Rehabilitation Act of 1973 — covering reasonable accommodations for deaf and hard-of-hearing — from the Title VI Civil Rights Act of 1964, which provides reasonable modifications to limited English proficiency (LEP) persons.

On August 16, 2000, President Bill Clinton signed Executive Order 13166, improving access to services for LEP persons. As a result, and by the authority vested in the President by the Constitution and the laws of the United States of America, LEP persons participating in federally funded and assisted programs are entitled to meaningful access to effectively communicate their needs for services without a fee or charge.

Thanks to the United States Department of Justice, enforcement of both the ADA/504 Rehabilitation Act of 1973 and Title VI of the Civil Rights Act of 1964 helps to prevent (disability and national origin) discrimination against deaf, hard-of-hearing and LEP individuals.

Credentials of the Author

+ Master's Degree in Public Administration with Concentration in Criminal Justice Administration
+ Bachelor's Degree in Management Organization Development
+ Served in city, county and state governments
+ Licensed Private Investigator

- Civil Rights Investigator for a well-known university
- Behavioral Health Clinician/Case Coordinator
- Section 504/ADA Coordinator
- Regional Language Access Coordinator
- Certified Forensic Interviewer
- Sexual Assault Investigations
- Domestic Violence Subject Matter Expert
- Rape Crisis Center
- Human Trafficking Board
- Refugee Task Force
- Certified Court Mediator (Alternate Dispute Resolution)
- Adjunct Instructor (Law Enforcement in the 21st Century)
- Community Officer Policing Streets (C.O.P.S) Program
- Juvenile Intervention Prevention Program Coordinator
- Graduate of Flint Police Academy
- Graduate of Florida Juvenile Justice Academy
- Graduate of Michigan Department of Corrections Academy

> If we desire respect
> for the law, we must
> first make the law
> respectable.
>
> *Louis D. Brandies*

Legal Aspects

The American Disabilities Act prohibits discrimination on the basis of disability in employment, state and local government, public accommodations, commercial facilities, transportation and telecommunications. It also applies to the United States Congress.

To be protected by the ADA, one must have a disability or have a relationship or association with an individual with a disability. An individual with a disability is defined by the ADA as a person who has a physical or mental impairment that substantially limits one or more major activities, a person who has a history or record of such an impairment, or a person who is perceived by others as having such an impairment. The ADA does not specifically name all of the impairments that are covered.

On one hand, Title VI of the Civil Rights Act of 1964 prohibits individuals from being excluded from participation in, denied the benefits of, or being subjected to discrimination under any program or activity receiving federal funds on the basis of race, color or national origin.

On the other hand, on August 16, 2010, Assistant Attorney General Tom Perez issued a language access guidance (letter to state courts) but the letter does not specifically address administrative adjudicative hearings conducted by state or local executive branch agencies that receive federal financial assistance. (**45 Code of Federal Regulations (C.F.R.), Part 80 and 42 U.S.C. 2000d et. seq.**)

Although ADA/Section 504 of the 1973 Rehabilitation Act protects qualified individuals from discrimination on the basis of disability, it only applies to agencies and organizations receiving federal funds. (**45 C.F.R. Part 84 and 29 U.S.C. 794**)

Americans with Disabilities Act of 1990-Title II protects qualified individuals from discrimination on the basis of disability. (**28 C.F.R. Part 35 and 42 U.S.C. 12131**)

Title VI Prohibitions

* Denying any individual services, opportunities or other benefits, for which that individual is otherwise qualified because of their race, color, or national origin

- Providing any service in a different manner from that which is provided to others in a program because of race, color or national origin

- Segregating clients solely because of race, color or national origin

- Restricting access to services because of race, color or national origin

- Adopting methods of administration which would limit participation by any group of recipients or subject them to discrimination

- Addressing an individual in a manner that denotes inferiority because of race, color or national origin

These prohibitions improve services to LEP clients receiving services offered by the public and other recipients and subrecipients receiving federal funds.

The improved services constitute a reasonable modification as opposed to a reasonable accommodation. A modification usually makes something work better or acts as change to eliminate barriers. An accommodation provides assistance as needed to a person with a disability.

The differences between an accommodation and a modification would be the laws covering the deaf and hard-of-hearing versus LEP individuals in the ADA/Rehabilitation Act of 1973 and Title VI Civil Rights Act of 1964.

As a reminder, the ADA/Rehabilitation Act addresses major life activities including caring for oneself; and performing manual tasks such as walking, seeing, concentrating and interacting with others. Other examples include sitting, standing, breathing, hearing and lifting; and mental and emotional processes such as speaking, learning and working. Title VI specifically lays out meaningful access for services to LEP.

The ADA amendments of 2008 include episodic and other physiological impairments such as cognitive, intellectual and developmental disabilities. The Rehabilitation Act of 1973 intersects with ADA, specifically covers services to those who are deaf and hard-of-hearing or blind/low vision and provides an accessibility plan to auxiliary aids and services.

Empowering Persons with Disabilities 2.0 begins with deaf and hard-of-hearing disabilities and transitions into discussing LEP in order to promote a commitment to serve individuals free of charge in programs and activities.

In this booklet, I discuss an effective service delivery model that can be applied in public agencies, community-based care (CBC) partnerships and private entities receiving federal assistance from public entities.

The booklet also gives tips for servicing persons with disabilities, addresses the four-factor analysis for LEP persons seeking services from covered entities and briefly touches on remote interpreting as an appropriate and reasonable alternative in a variety of circumstances.

Likewise, I offer information on qualified in-person interpreters, the benefit of using remote technology, the nature and duration of the proceeding or communication, along with costs and delays associated with in-person and remote interpreters as a benefit for compliance.

I hear with my eyes
and speak with my
hands.

Waleska "Jai" Velez

Knowing How to Assist the Deaf and Hard-of-Hearing

The tips and tools presented for dealing with sensory disabilities are universal and shall serve as a model of effective communication with persons who are deaf or hard-of-hearing. In particular, the use of auxiliary aids and services are essential because it allows such persons equal opportunities to participate in and enjoy the benefits of a service, program or activity.

A discussion of auxiliary aids and services is an appropriate step to having a sound policy for the deaf and hard-of-hearing.

Here are some tips:

+ Determine what a client's preferred method of communication is and provide a certified interpreter for sign language access; for example, Haitian Creole, French Creole, Portuguese, Spanish, English or others.

✦ Note-taking can be used to establish their preferred method of communication, but this should be limited.

✦ If an entity hosts a community event involving the public and clients, it is best to use a Communication Access Real-Time Transcription (CART) provider.

The transcriptionist is similar to a court stenographer, but the CART provider will be assisted by at least 2 or 3 sign language interpreters to interpret in real time.

The transcription service uses a stenotype machine, computer and screen projector in real time, along with software to instantly translate speech into readable text for a seamless captioning experience. A CART provider would be fitting for a group of deaf clients in need of services.

This process could be applied for taking depositions, in focus groups, conferences and teleconferences.

Other aids would be:

✦ Telephone handset amplifiers

✦ Assistive listening devices. i.e., Pocket talkers

- Video conferencing captioning tools Zoom/ITS Documentation

- Note takers may be helpful but should be limited to establishing a preferred method of communication.

- Use of closed caption decoders, open and closed captioning tools are helpful for clients waiting for services.

The reason for focusing on deaf and hard-of-hearing (DHH) auxiliary aids is because private and public sectors within the medical profession, community-based care (CBC), behavioral health clinicians, first responders and frontline employees are more likely to have contact with DHH persons. In many cases, deaf persons are illiterate to languages spoken by the hearing community, both in lip-reading and writing.

Deaf people are born into a world rich with language, but parents may not know that their infant child is deaf. The first words are usually spoken by age one. Barring serious neurocognitive impairments, children will have mastered their native language(s) by approximately age five.

If deafness of a child is detected between ages one and six it is known as prelingual deafness. If the deafness of a child occurs after age six, then it is post-lingual. The term for a person who becomes deaf as an adult is "late-deafened."

The acquisition of proficiency in whatever language and the experience of gaining access to that language is essential to other developmental domains such as cognition, social-emotional skills, school readiness and academic outcomes.

A deaf child's perceptual inabilities and family language environment, including lack of exposure to sign language, often result in a lack of easily-accessible language input for the child. Deprivation of sign language or signing sufficient to support the person's full first language at an appropriate stage may impact development of the child.

Deaf people impacted at either an early age or as adults are led to find their own deaf community to learn from, which affects their literacy rate for both reading and writing. The rate of literacy may also decline for those who are hard-of-hearing.

Understanding the Loss of Hearing

Hearing loss categories include auditory, conductive, sensorineural and mixed hearing loss.

+ Auditory processing disorders occur when the brain has problems processing information contained in sound, such as understanding speech and determining where sounds are coming from.

* Conductive hearing loss occurs when there is a problem with the outer or middle ear which interferes with passing sound to the inner ear. It can be caused by such things as too much ear wax, ear infections, a punctured eardrum, fluid build-up or abnormal bone growth in the middle ear.

* Sensorineural hearing loss occurs when the hearing organ —cochlea — and/or the auditory nerve — organ of Corti — are damaged or malfunction, so they are unable to accurately send electrical information to the brain. Sensorineural hearing loss is almost always permanent.

The importance of treating a deaf person as an individual and not a disability is critical to improving their lives.

Hubert Humphrey, speaking on the treatment of those with disabilities, said, "The moral test of government is how that government treats those who are in the dawn of life, the children; those who are in the twilight of life, the elderly; and those who are in the shadows of life, the sick, the needy and the handicapped."

These tips — applied by law enforcement, behavioral health clinicians, other public and private agencies and their contract service providers for service delivery — will help us pass that test.

Assisting Persons who are Deaf or Hard-of-Hearing

In traumatic situations with individuals who are deaf or hard-of-hearing, it is critical to find out their preferred method of communicating. They may need a sign language interpreter, but how does one ask?

+ First, establish a short distance between yourself and the individual — 4 to 6 feet — when speaking directly to them.

+ Note writing may be helpful to establish their preferred method of communication, but it must be limited to short phrases. "Do you sign in English?" "Do you sign in Creole?" "Do you sign in Spanish?"

+ Some deaf people will ask to communicate by notes. Be careful! Note writing and lip reading should not substitute as acceptable communication.

+ It is critical to understand that not every deaf individual can read lips. If you attempt lip reading, it must be to establish the deaf individual's preferred method of communications, such as sign language.

+ Avoid raising your voice as an alternative to lip reading.

+ If you choose lip reading, look at the person, speak clearly in short phrases and slowly enunciate the words in natural progression.

+ Use I-Speak flashcards with words, phrases, objects or drawing of essential needs such as food or water.

+ Again, rudimentary styles of communication such as lip reading and note writing to ask questions should be used only to determine what their preferred method of communication will be for the service delivery. Be prepared to repeat yourself.

+ In response to a traumatic event, deaf people may express themselves with gestures and movements that seem agitated or aggressive. Remember, it may be their interest in getting help.

+ For the individual and the service provider, it is critical to use appropriate auxiliary aids and services. The purpose of a certified interpreter is to ensure victims that are deaf or hard-of-hearing receive the appropriate information for services.

+ Deaf or hard-of-hearing persons may want their child or another person under 18 to communicate for them because of personal relationships. Respectfully decline that request and get a certified interpreter for them and you. If that family member or friend misinterprets what occurred, it is likely that information will impact outcomes.

* Should a deaf individual ask the provider to use a personal friend or relative over age 18, it is permissible, but they should only be used to establish the individual's preferred method of communication and biographical and demographic information.

* In some instances, a provider can use video remote interpreting (VRI) which benefits the victim with disabilities at the point of contact.

* A VRI interpreter is often available within minutes for scheduled virtual visits and within two hours for unscheduled visits. The interaction and interpretation may occur via smart phone or desktop or laptop computer. All are highly desirable interpersonal options to provide immediate language support. The meeting occurs between the deaf individual, the service provider, and certified interpreter in a private setting.

* Another method of communicating with individuals with disabilities is Video Relay. (A search for video relay interpreters will lead to different vendors.) The individual with disabilities initiates contact with a video relay operator, and that operator will call a land line or cell phone to establish contact between all parties.

Tips for Using Video Remote Interpreting

An in-person interpreter is considered the gold standard, but environmental concerns, medical conditions or other accommodations can affect the use of an interpreter who comes to the agency. Here are some advantages for using remote technology.

+ Services can be obtained by cell phone for compliance.

+ Use of VRI 24/7 enables response in minutes.

+ Enhanced accuracy for visual support

+ On-demand interpreting solutions for the primary language

+ Cost effectiveness (over-the-phone versus on-site interpreting)

Tips for Using the Video Relay System

+ If a video relay system is the choice, it is critical to wait for the VR operator to introduce themselves with their operator ID. Such an exchange may occur in this manner: "Hello, this is Video Relay Operator 73285, and I have Dennis on the line." The service provider may want to ask the VR operator to repeat their ID if they did not catch it the first time, and then speak directly to Dennis about his concern(s).

✦ The VR operator serves as the intermediary for the service provider and deaf person. The process allows all parties to participate to help the deaf person.

✦ Actively listen to the victim with disabilities, refer to them by name when speaking and don't interrupt the operator or deaf person.

✦ If it appears that an agreement will not be reached on the issue, attempt to find a point of agreement and ask the victim if they would like you to refer them to someone who can better help them. Before the call ends, ask if there is anything else you can do for them.

Tips for Using a Certified Interpreter in Person

✦ If an interpreter is contacted, make sure they are certified and registered with the National Registry of Interpreters for the Deaf by searching www.rid.org for identification.

✦ If the interpreter's ID is unavailable on rid.org, you may want to ask if the interpreter has a block on their home address which may prevent their ID from being found. If they are not listed on rid.org, the interpreter is less likely to be certified and should not be used.

+ A service provider may be tempted to use a co-worker who has taken minimal sign language classes. This is risky and prohibited if it will be substituted for using a certified interpreter.

+ In cases of maltreatment of the client, time is of the essence, and auxiliary aids and services must be delivered quickly, which means one must ensure an appropriate accommodation is available for the encounter.

+ In some cases, deaf individuals wear hearing aids but are still unable to hear clearly. If you observe a hearing aid, it may be to enable them to accentuate tones or pitches when others speak. Do not assume they can hear in detail.

+ There are times when more than one member of a family may need assistance. If appropriate services are in place, then one may use a CART provider.

+ For the hard-of-hearing, one may use assistive listening devices (ALD), which can serve up to 20 persons in a classroom setting. They come with neck-loops and ADA plaques. Another is a Pocket Talker, or frequency modulation (FM) system.

+ An ALD may be used with Cochlear implants or hearing aids to help a wearer hear sounds and tones.

+ If a certified interpreter or an ALD is not available, reschedule the services to accommodate the individual who is deaf.

Exercise 1: A deaf individual with limited experience using sign language visits a service provider. The service provider has one year of high school in American Sign Language interpreting for the deaf. Which of the following should the service provider do?

A) Interpret to help find out what services the provider can offer.

B) Take notes and watch the deaf individual's facial expression to see if they understand.

C) Take notes and write down short phrases to determine the deaf individual's preferred method of communication?

If you chose C, you are taking the right steps to help deaf or hard-of-hearing persons to get the services they need.

Exercise 2: An interpreting vendor is contacted, and the agency sends an interpreter within an hour. The service provider is excited about the quick arrival because it is an unexpected appointment. The deaf individual begins signing and the interpreter signs back. After a few minutes, the deaf person begins looking frustrated. Which of the following should the service provider do?

A) Allow the interpreter to continue and explain to the deaf individual that the interpreter is from a credible agency.

B) Immediately stop the session, ask the interpreter for their RID identification number, ask the deaf individual if they understand, and then call the vendor.

C) Document what occurred and reschedule the services.

If you selected B and C, you are correct. It is important to ask the interpreter for their ID before the services begin. If you forget, it's okay to request it at any time. They may not be certified. Check rid.org and call the vendor to report what occurred, then document it.

The impact of incidents like this to victims with disabilities must not be minimized. Apologize and communicate in short phrases with the client. Ask if they would like another interpreter. If so, contact another vendor. You may have to ask the client to reschedule.

Scenario: A Child Protective Service (CPS) worker is investigating an allegation of child abuse. The alleged perpetrator is the mother, who is deaf. The victim is her child, who is deaf as well. The CPS worker visited the home without a certified interpreter.

The CPS worker decided to interview the mother without a certified interpreter by using hand-written notes. The interview lasted for hours.

Although the CPS worker did not interview the child, he concluded the child had been abused and obtained support from his CPS supervisor for removal. The child became tearful and loud during separation. This continued in three different foster homes.

The mother contacted an advocacy group, which provided an attorney to address the investigation, particularly the hand-written notes.

A court hearing ensued. The court provided its own certified interpreter and determined that the mother's account conflicted with the CPS worker's notes and did not amount to abuse.

The court ordered CPS to locate the child and bring him to court. The mishandling of the case led to a delay due to the number of homes the child had been taken to. The court was furious because of the trauma to the child, and advocates pushed for policy changes.

Here are changes you may be required to make:

+ Establish a Request for Services/Waiver Form. The form would include the name of the deaf client and the services requested or declined.

✦ Create a form for Communication Assistance to ensure documentation outlining the deaf person's access to their preferred method of communication, the type of auxiliary aid provided, (for instance, ALD, certified interpreter, note taker, CART provider, etc.), and their disability; i.e., deaf, hard-of-hearing, low vision or blind.

✦ Create a survey form and give the form to the deaf or hard-of-hearing individual to submit to the covered entity, and not the individual completing the services. The form is to be mailed by the deaf individual to a neutral location.

This service delivery model used allows for self-reporting and could work in a number of fields if it becomes policy.

There's none so blind
as those who will
not listen.

Neil Gaimon

Visually Impaired

The same processes are applied for the blind/low vision or visually impaired. However, here are tips unique to providing services to individuals who are blind or have low vision.

+ Ensure the individual with a visual impairment knows your name and agency and that the service provider documents the services requested.

+ Be aware that an increase in other senses is common in persons with a visual impairment. It is crucial to not speak loudly, but with a normal voice; this will help the process flow much better. Use your speech, assistive technology and a careful choice of words to indicate concern for their well-being, as well as to remain engaged throughout the process.

+ Avoid touching or trying to physically assist a blind/low vision person without asking their permission. It is better to ask if they would like you to escort them to the area of service. If so, extend your arm, hand, or elbow.

+ If it is necessary for an individual to move to an object such as a desk, tell them it is X steps away to their left, right, front or rear or by clock hours, with 12 o'clock being directly in front of them. Example: "The chair is five steps behind you at 4 o'clock."

+ Often individuals who are blind or partially sighted have service dogs to accommodate their disability. It is extremely important not to engage the animal as though it is a pet. Never pet the animal.

+ When escorting a visually impaired person, give prompts about where you are going, what the next door leads to or what the area you will be entering contains.

+ Since the blind or partially sighted person came for services, ask if they read braille and be prepared to offer adjusted writing guides for blind or low vision. The writing guide can be adjusted to the desired width by sliding the right margin from side to side. Its built-in notches along the upper track holds the margin guide in place.

+ The writing guide measures 9 3/8 by 1 1/2 inches and weighs 1.6 ounces. There are notches to hold forms in place for their signature.

- Offer to fill out the forms for them. Explain each document and why the form is legally required by ADA and Section 504.

- It is critical to follow the policy of your agency by documenting the initial contact, demeanor of the client and the content of your conversation. This is helpful in establishing what occurred without relying solely on your interpretation.

- A scribe assistant could be an individual in the office to help you complete the paperwork.

- Avoid lapses of conversation during the interview and inform the client if you are going to be silent for a time.

Being disabled should
not mean being
disqualified from
having access to every
aspect of life.

Emma Thompson

Do's and Don'ts of
Service Delivery (ADA/504)

+ Providing notice in the form of posters, client brochures, handbooks and consent forms frequently encountered in the population served should be noted.

+ Communicate with the client in the client's preferred language. This may require your agency to contract with a qualified interpreter if one is not available.

+ You cannot charge the client for an interpreter's services.

+ You cannot require the client to bring someone to interpret for them or use a minor child to interpret.

Empowering People With Disablities 2.0

+ You must provide notice to clients of their right to interpreters, free of charge.

+ You must provide clients with contact information to file a discrimination complaint with the agency and/or DOJ-Office of Civil Rights, if you believe discrimination occurred.

Disability doesn't
make you exceptional,
but questioning what
you think you know
about it does.

Stella Young

Americans with Disabilities Act of 1990 (ADA) Title II

ADA is a Federal Civil Rights Statute that prohibits discrimination against people with disabilities. It was designed to remove barriers that prevent people with disabilities from enjoying the same opportunities that are available to people without disabilities.

Tips on developing an Auxiliary Aids/Accessibility Plan

Auxiliary Aids Plans — also known as "Accessibility Plans" — are designed to be a resource for all staff. It is the "go to" plan for staff that ensures compliance.

Remember: Staff cannot utilize an Auxiliary Aids/Accessibility Plan if they do not know it exists!

The plan cites your organization's policies for assisting clients with impairments or interpreter needs.

It sets out in detail how to secure a sign language interpreter or a foreign-language interpreter and instructs staff how to access Relay Service.

It may include a list of bilingual staff members and their contact information.

The plan asserts that employees must obtain appropriate aids to ensure communication accommodation in the field and the office.

Employees must have an interpreter with a client when interviewing or communicating with an individual with hearing impairment

The plan also contains lists and locations of:

+ Certified and qualified interpreters
+ Assistive listening devices and systems
+ State Relay Services (They have 3-digit numbers, e.g. 411, 711)
+ VRI and VRS technology
+ Qualified readers
+ Braille and large print materials
+ Video tapes, teletypewriters (TTY/TDD) transcriptions, taped text

+ Any similar device or service that is needed to make spoken or aural language accessible is also considered an auxiliary aid.

Points to Consider in Auxiliary Aids and Services Plans

+ Method of communication most comfortable for client, e.g., written, flash cards or sign language
+ Length of communication
+ Number of persons involved
+ Purpose of communication
+ Complexity of information being communicated

Tips on using Qualified/ Certified Interpreters

A qualified interpreter is a person able to interpret effectively, accurately and impartially; both receptively and expressively, using specialized vocabulary required by the circumstance.

A certified interpreter is a person who has attended and passed the required educational and certification process.

Service Delivery to Hearing Impaired or Blind

Auxiliary aids include:

+ Certified interpreters, assistive listening systems (loop FM and infrared); television captioning and decoders; and video tapes, both open and closed captioned.

+ Any similar device or service that is needed to make spoken or aural language accessible is also considered an auxiliary aid.

+ If a blind/low vision person needs your help, consider asking an assistant to transcribe the document, and reader(s), or an individual could use taped texts, Braille and large print materials as auxiliary aids.

Follow your Agency and Region's Auxiliary Aids/ Accessibility Plan for circuit-specific protocol.

+ An organization must incorporate an interpreter, translator, and may consider recruiting, hiring, or incentivizing employees to play a role in building an effective accessibility plan.

+ Remember, the plan is to provide a service and should be free of charge to the client.

+ If time permits, obtain an interpreter prior to initial contact.

+ If time does not permit obtaining an interpreter prior to initial contact — i.e. hotline immediate response calls — utilize other means of providing services such as a paid service called The Language Line, which provides the organization with enumerable foreign language translators.

+ Establish a contract with agencies that have qualified interpreters and make it a part of your budget.

Supervisors' Responsibilities to Service Delivery

A Contracted Service Provider (CSP) is a person or an agency that contracts with a public agency or 501c3 non-profit to provide the amount and kind of services requested by the agency, or provides services under the contract to beneficiaries individually determined to be eligible by the agency. It is the supervising agency's responsibility to:

+ Ensure CSP staff provides accommodations such as auxiliary aids for the deaf, hard-of-hearing and vision-impaired clients.

+ Ensure that all staff are trained and are aware of the Circuit/Region's Auxiliary Aids/Accessibility Plan.

+ Ensure that all potential and actual CSP clients are treated in a nondiscriminatory manner.

✦ Deaf and hard-of-hearing must have equal access to services. Effective communication can be provided through certified bilingual staff.

✦ Clients must be informed about and provided with free interpreter or translation services as necessary to ensure equal access.

✦ Sign Language and Sign System are visual or tactile ways of communicating thoughts, ideas and feelings through American Sign Language (ASL) or manual signs and gestures with specifically defined vocabulary.

✦ Primary Language is the language identified by the client as the language in which he or she prefers to communicate; ASL, Spanish, Creole, etc.

✦ If there is a breakdown in communication, and you need to reschedule the visit, the steps attempted to secure a translator or interpreter should be documented, and the client must be informed of the earliest appointment for an interpreter.

✦ In non-emergency cases, obtain the services of an interpreter prior to the scheduled visit, appointment, staffing or meeting.

Limited English Proficiency:

Using the Four-Factor Analysis to Determine the Organization's Obligation

This is the Four-Factor Analysis that comes with service delivery:

Factor 1: Number or proportion of LEP persons eligible to be served or likely to be affected by the program or service.

Potential sources of data include:

+ Encounter data

- Data from census, school systems, state and local government

- Community organizations

- Refugee/immigrant agencies

- Does the program serve minors whose parents/ guardians are LEP?

- Are there populations who may be underserved because of language barriers?

Factor 2: Frequency of Contact

- How often is a particular language encountered?

- The more frequent the contact with a particular group, the more likely language services are needed.

Factor 3: Nature and importance of the program, activity, or service

- How important is the recipient's activity, information, service, or program?

- What are the possible consequences if effective communication is not achieved?

- Could denial or delay of access to services or information have serious, life-threatening implications?

Factor 4: Cost and availability of resources

- No cost to the LEP individual

- Information sharing

Limited English Proficiency

+ Training bilingual staff
+ Telephone and video conference services
+ Pooling resources, standardizing documents
+ Using sufficiently qualified translators and interpreters to avoid errors and unnecessary costs
+ Centralizing services
+ Formalized use of qualified volunteers

Types of Oral Language Resources

+ Bilingual staff.
+ Contracted Interpreter Services
+ Volunteers
+ Telephone language line
+ Must not require clients to use family or friends or minor children

Written Translations

+ Translate documents into regularly encountered non-English languages.
+ Do this when a significant number or percentage of the eligible population is LEP and needs the services or information in a non-English language in order to communicate effectively.
+ Vital documents

- Application forms
- Consent forms
- Enrollment forms
- Rights and responsibilities
- Letters or notices about eligibility or change in benefits
- Anything that requires a response
- Medical or discharge information

All written materials are translated for each LEP group of 3000 or 10% (whichever is less) of the eligible population.

Vital documents are translated for each group of 1000 or 5% (whichever is less) of the eligible population.

For each language group with fewer than 100 persons, the service entity provides written notice of the right to receive oral interpretation of written materials in the primary language of the group.

Information must be provided in alternative formats for LEP persons, including Web-based information.

The required nondiscrimination statement must be included on all informational materials provided to the public.

The message of equal opportunity must be conveyed in all program-related information provided to the public, including photographs and other graphics.

The LEP Access Plan

The guidance for LEP under the Department of Justice (DOJ) Civil Division is to ensure that LEP individuals have meaningful access to programs and activities. Accordingly, all staff shall take reasonable steps to ensure LEP individuals are provided appropriate language assistance services and to inform the public of the availability of language accessible programs and activities.

Language assistance services and the persons or entities (providers) that offer such services generally fall into one or more of three groups.

The DOJ Civil Division states, "Barring exigent circumstances, the Division shall not use children, family, friends or bystanders of the LEP person to provide official language assitance services." Otherwise, children, family and bystanders should not be used to interpret or translate because it could result in a breach of confidentiality, a conflict of interest or an inadequate interpretation.

As referred to in the LEP Access Plan, "quality language assistance services" applies to language assistance services that facilitate meaningful access to programs and activities.

A practical guide to effective communication should include providers who specialize in interpretation, qualified interpreters, translation, qualified translators, and bilingual persons to ensure accurate and timely delivery of services.

With languages, you are at home anywhere.

Edward De Waal

Resources

Practical Guides On Effective Communication

Health Research and Educational Trust's (HRET) Disparities Toolkit (www.hretdisparities.org) This toolkit is designed to help health care organizations understand the importance of collecting accurate data on race, ethnicity and primary language of persons who have limited English proficiency and/or are deaf or hard-of-hearing.

Using this Toolkit, organizations can assess their capacity to collect language access information and implement a systematic framework designed specifically for obtaining race, ethnicity and primary language data directly from patients/enrollees or their caregivers in an efficient, effective and respectful manner.

Robert Wood Johnson Foundation's (RWJF) Speaking Together Toolkit (www.rwjf.org/qualitye quality/product .jsp?id=29653) This toolkit provides advice to hospitals on improving the quality and accessibility of their language services. The toolkit was developed as part of RWJF's Speaking Together: National Language Services. Network, which was a program involving ten hospitals that worked toward improving the availability and quality of language services for LEP populations.

NHeLP's Language Services Resource Guide for Health Care Providers (www.healthlaw.org/library/ item.118835) was developed to help healthcare eliminate disparities to patients. The toolkit is guidance from The Joint Commision related to effective communication.

The language services guide was developed to aid health care providers, administrators, interpreters, translators and others in improving language access and improving health care for their clients and patients. The guide gathers basic information about providing language services in one document. Information includes interpreter and translator associations and agencies, training programs, assessment tools, and other materials.

HHS Office on Minority Health; A Patient-Centered Guide to Implementing Language Access Services in Healthcare Organizations (www. omhrc.gov/assets/pdf/checked/hc-lsig.pdf) This guide is intended to help academia and healthcare organizations implement effective language access services to meet the needs of their LEP clients and patients to increase their access to health care.

Title VI creates an environment where staff and patients from diverse backgrounds can communicate better as it relates to effective service delivery models for limited English proficient clients.

American Medical Association's Ethical Force Program's Improving Communication — Improving Care (www.ethicalforce.org) This is a consensus report by the Ethical Force Program that helps health care organizations prioritize effective communication and create environments where staff members and patients can effectively communicate about improving the quality of life.

The Office for Civil Rights' Policy Guidance for Title VI (www.hhs.gov/ocr/lep) This website provides guidance on Title VI as it relates to LEP populations.

The guidance offers an overview of who is covered, basic requirements, definitions of key terms, possible methods for providing meaningful access, examples of frequently encountered scenarios, promising practices, a model language assistance program plan and enforcement issues. When properly established, the service delivery model will create an effective policy.

The Office for Civil Rights' Effective Communication webpage (www.hhs.gov/ocr/hospital communication.html) provides healthcare providers with tools that assist people with limited English proficiency and people who are deaf or hard-of-hearing.

To help hospitals meet the communication needs of LEP, deaf, or hard-of-hearing patients, this site provides information and resources on how to effectively communicate to improve Patient-Provider Communications regardless of race, color, national origin, and disability. The resources are related to Title VI, Section 504/ADA for service delivery.

Department of Justice's ADA Business Brief (www.ada.gov/hospcombr.htm)

The service delivery model provides an overview of what organizations should expect when monitored as required under the guidance of the Joint Commission and HHS. Likewise, the accessibility plan creates the terms for communicating with people who are deaf or hard-of-hearing and LEP persons within an organization.

National Health Law Programs (NHeLP) Summary of State Law Requirements Addressing Language Needs in Health Care (www.healthlaw.

org/library/item.174993) This publication outlines each state's statutes and regulations regarding services to LEP persons in health care settings. The high-quality language access services create an environment to utilize a wider range of healthcare services to individuals with limited English proficiency (LEP) and eliminates barriers.

The Office of Minority Health's National Standards for Culturally and Linguistically Appropriate Services (www.omhrc.gov/clas) supports healthcare outcomes if LEP persons are unable to speak or read and ensures language access.

These national standards were developed to encourage health care organizations and individual providers to make their practices more culturally and linguistically accessible. The standards address issues such as cultural competence, linguistically appropriate services and organizational supports for cultural competence.

International Medical Interpreters Association and Education Development Center, Inc.; Medical Interpreting Standards of Practice (www.imiaweb. org/uploads/pages/102.pdf) These standards of practice were developed to be a vital evaluation and competency tool for professional interpreters all over the country, delineating core performance standards and competencies required of a "competent" interpreter.

National Council on Interpreting in Health Care's National Standards of Practice for Interpreters in Health Care (www.ncihc.org) is composed of leaders from around the country who work as medical interpreters, interpreter service coordinators and trainers, clinicians, and policy makers.

The standards of practice are intended to be used as a reference by interpreters and those who work with, train and employ interpreters. They are intended to guide the practice of all interpreters and to acquaint non-interpreters with the standards recognized within the interpreting profession.

These efforts help to identify the urgency of the problem or issue taking into account the standard practice of ethics, patient autonomy, and formulate possible plans of action.

National Heath Law Program's Language Access in Health Care Statement of Principles. This Statement of Principles springs from the work of numerous national organizations to develop an agenda to improve policies and funding for access to health care for LEP persons. The intent is to provide a broad framework to inform efforts to improve health care delivered to LEP individuals.

Conclusion

The Review Process

Empowering persons with disabilities must include an evaluation of the service delivery model, and appropriate feedback in an inclusive environment. The goal to help persons with disabilities requires the input of the administration, managers, supervisor, professionals, staff and contractors.

I have had the honor of providing training, information and education (T.I.E.) to 12 state facilities and 269 contractors or subcontractors. The recipients and sub-recipients of federal funds were required to provide services to limited English proficient persons and DHH clients.

My efforts began with providing training and concluded with monitoring for compliance. Here are the steps that I took to help these organizations:

First, I identified those receiving federal funding assistance.

Second, I reviewed a list of organizations that had formal complaints filed within 24 months.

Third, I searched for organizations that failed to report monthly, quarterly or annual records showing services to the DHH or LEP clients.

Issues identified triggered an Entrance Inspection, an Entrance Interview, Staff Interviews, File Reviews, and an Exit Interview.

Entrance Inspection: Walking into a higher-education institution, healthcare organization or a facility that has subcontractors requires notice, but that may be negated if an immediate response is required. Otherwise, 30- to 45-day notice should be given to the organization. In any case, it is proper to give notice.

On the date of review, I start by coming through the entrance used by the public and look for three 11-by-17-inch posters visible in conspicuous locations on a bulletin board or wall.

One poster should be dedicated to the DHH and contain information about how to access these free services.

The second poster should be for LEP persons and contain various languages for accessibility and free translation services.

The third poster provides patients/clients with the appropriate laws indicating why these services are required.

The LEP and DHH posters must have contact information of the organization's coordinator, should an individual need to report an issue. Generally, such a report would be discussed with the Single Point of Contact (SPOC) or his or her designee.

If the posters are not present, found in conspicuous locations and/or don't meet the required 11-by-17-inch guidelines for readers, it will be discussed in the entrance interview.

Entrance Interview: The meeting with administrators often occurs during this interview. During the interview phase, I begin by reviewing the Equal Employment Opportunities (EEO) policies to determine if the employer has written policies to protect applicants, employees and clients from discrimination. Since it gives workers and their families a fair shot to reach their highest dreams and aspirations, it helps to determine if those with disabilities are included.

I also review the grievance procedures to ensure employees and clients have an outlet to express concerns, complaints or alleged violations, as well as follow the process for resolving their issues.

During the interview, I specifically ask questions related to the types of services provided to clients, and whether there are employees with similar disabilities or limited English proficient, who are similarly situated and treated differently.

Additionally, I speak with a percentage of employees currently on shift and ask if the agency has any clients available who are willing to share their experiences with me. The conversation helps to identify the client(s) with file(s) to sample and to select staff for interviews.

Staff Interviews: The model of randomly selecting staff is often based on the availability and/or number of staff currently working.

The staff selected from the roster are escorted by another staff member into a private area, and asked to participate in the process.

Each staff member is asked the same questions and offered a scenario or two to determine whether they have taken any training on how to effectively communicate with LEP and DHH persons. This also allows me to ask about encounters they may have had with client(s) recently interviewed or an employee that requires language access or auxiliary aids and services.

The questions are not intended to be a test, but serve as an opportunity to determine if the administration has proactively implemented their policy and procedures and documented these services.

I have had the opportunity to interview clients and I have used video conferencing with translators or an interpreter to facilitate the interview. The success of using these auxiliary aids have led to disclosures and identifying files that contained errors.

File Reviews: The file reviews depend on the population served at that institution but if files are centralized and the institution has other facilities, then the sample size may increase.

During the review, I commonly look for the appropriate forms the institution should be using. If the forms are absent or improperly completed, I document the concerns. I also look for documentation from staff about encounters with clients, and determine if staff members used the appropriate language. For instance, I found that one client who had trouble hearing had asked for an assisted listening device, but the staff member wrote, "The (name inserted) could hear out of the other ear."

It is appropriate at this stage to compare the information received from the entrance inspection, entrance interviews, staff interviews and client interviews to address the errors made when delivering services.

The compiled information and documentation creates an opportunity to discuss the concerns in the closing phase or exit interview.

Exit Interview: The exit interview is to discuss the overall compliance review that occurs on the last day of the inspection and it can be performed via Zoom.

In this phase, I refer back to the policy and procedures, and remind administrators of the questions I asked earlier and the response given before the review. The gentle reminder allows me to offer suggestions about the organizations accessibility/auxiliary aids plan.

In some cases, I ask the administrator to consider using the four-factors analysis as discussed earlier. In others, I strongly recommend using other types of documents to capture LEP information, rather than using the same forms used for deaf and hard-of-hearing persons, and provide suggestions.

The discussion will also highlight findings at each stage, if any, and provide recommendations for meaningful access to ensure effective communication or the development of accessibility plan for the hearing impaired.

During the exit interview, I inform the organization that I plan on visiting the issues discussed within 30 days or suggest conducting a desk review to ensure all errors are rectified to help the organization build on their success.

In all cases, I contact the organization's SPOC to close out the review and ask that person to join a bi-weekly or monthly video or phone conference for updates. The SPOC meeting will give the representative of that entity an opportunity to prepare for future compliance as well as ask questions to ensure self-reporting ahead of monitoring.

In closing the review process, I take the opportunity to help the organization with their posters, provide a list of vendors and various technologies to reduce cost for the free services. If the organization makes an effort to correct deficiencies, it reduces the likelihood of corrective action.

The Title VI compliance methods that I present have been used in the past, and should be applied in part or whole when measuring the objectives of providing LEP services and auxiliary aids and services to clients. At best, they are components used by others, and may serve as monitoring tools to help service providers remain in compliance.

This handbook places emphasis on the deaf and hard-of-hearing (sensory) and language access for LEP individuals as a service model to effectively communicate.

The model also points out the legal aspects to reduce liability when a covered agency or contractors deliver services to LEP persons and deaf and hard-of-hearing individuals. This practical guide can be used in the public and the private sector, but it is best used when implemented in policy, procedures, and training development.

The application of this guide removes barriers to race, color, sex, gender and those with disabilities.

The Language Access Assessment and Planning Tool for Federally Conducted and Federally Assisted Programs requires compliance from covered entities. For purposes of enforcement, Attorney General Eric Holder issued a Memorandum to all Federal Agencies regarding Executive Order 13166 on February 17, 2011.

The guidance offered by AG Holder stated, "Whether in an emergency or in the course of routine business matters, the success of government efforts to effectively communicate with members of the public depends on the widespread and nondiscriminatory availability of accurate, timely, and vital information."

It is recommended that organizations or recipients and sub-recipients receiving federal funding use the appropriate service providers to deliver auxiliary aids and services to LEP persons and DHH clients.

Any time you think
some other language is
strange, remember that
yours is just as strange;
you're just used to it.

Anonymous

Empowering People With Disablities 2.0

Acknowledgements

Sandy Compton and Blue Creek Press worked closely with me and frequently offered updates on the production of this booklet. I highly recommend Sandy and Blue Creek Press to anyone looking to get published.

I dedicate this book to Jai Velez because she inspired me to offer tips on communicating with the Deaf and Hard-of-hearing community. Jai is deaf, and truly hears with her eyes and speaks with her hands.

Jai, you are an incredible person, and your life experiences have breathed life into others. I believe you have a story to tell and that is enough to live for. Patty and I love you. Thank you!

www.ingramcontent.com/pod-product-compliance
Lightning Source LLC
Chambersburg PA
CBHW060520280326
41933CB00014B/3048